C
9/08

Learn to Draw
MACHINES

MEDIA ENHANCED BOOKS

AV2 BY WEIGL™

ADDED VALUE • AUDIO VISUAL

www.av2books.com

AV² provides enriched content that supplements and complements this book. Weigl's AV² books strive to create inspired learning and engage young minds in a total learning experience.

Your AV² Media Enhanced books come alive with...

Audio
Listen to sections of the book read aloud.

Key Words
Study vocabulary, and complete a matching word activity.

Video
Watch informative video clips.

Quizzes
Test your knowledge.

Go to **www.av2books.com**, and enter this book's unique code.

Embedded Weblinks
Gain additional information for research.

Slide Show
View images and captions, and prepare a presentation.

BOOK CODE

K289972

Try This!
Complete activities and hands-on experiments.

... and much, much more!

AV² by Weigl brings you media enhanced books that support active learning.

Published by AV² by Weigl
350 5ᵗʰ Avenue, 59ᵗʰ Floor
New York, NY 10118
Website: www.weigl.com   www.av2books.com

Library of Congress Cataloging-in-Publication Data

Machines / edited by Jordan McGill.
    p. cm. -- (Learn to draw)
Includes index.
ISBN 978-1-61690-858-4 (hardcover : alk. paper) -- ISBN 978-1-61690-864-5 (pbk. : alk. paper) -- ISBN 978-1-61690-988-8 (online)
1. Motor vehicles in art--Juvenile literature. 2. Drawing--Technique--Juvenile literature. I. McGill, Jordan.
NC825.M64M33 2011
743'.996218--dc23
                              2011020312

Printed in the United States of America in North Mankato, Minnesota
1 2 3 4 5 6 7 8 9 0 15 14 13 12 11

062011
WEP290411

Project Coordinator: Jordan McGill
Art Director: Terry Paulhus

Every reasonable effort has been made to trace ownership and to obtain permission to reprint copyright material. The publishers would be pleased to have any errors or omissions brought to their attention so that they may be corrected in subsequent printings.

Weigl acknowledges Getty Images as its primary image supplier for this title.

Contents

6

10

14

18

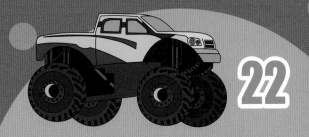

22

26

Why Draw?

Drawing is easier than you think. Look around you. The world is made of shapes and lines. By combining simple shapes and lines anything can be drawn. An orange is just a circle with a few details added. A flower can be a circle with ovals drawn around it. An ice cream cone can be a triangle topped with a circle. Most anything, no matter how complicated, can be broken down into simple shapes.

oval

circle

circle

circle

triangle

Drawing helps people make sense of the world. It is a way to reduce an object to its simplest form, say our most personal feelings and thoughts, or show others objects from our **imagination**. Drawing an object can help you learn how it fits together and works.

What shapes do you see in this car?

It is fun to put the world onto a page, but it is also a good way to learn. Learning to draw even simple objects introduces the skills needed to fully express oneself visually. Drawing is an excellent form of **communication** and improves people's imagination.

Practice drawing your favorite machines in this book to learn the basic skills necessary to draw. You can use those skills to create your own drawings.

Machines

Drawing machines is a useful way to learn how all their parts fit together and how they work. As you draw each part of the machines in this book, consider how each part works together. Think about how each part makes the machine useful.

People rely on all types of machines to make life easier and more enjoyable. Some of the most impressive machines are the mighty machines people use to help them complete large tasks or travel great distances.

Machines help people work faster and more effectively. They move people from one place to another. Without machines, people would not be able to travel around the world and transport goods overnight. Without machines, people could not raise huge skyscrapers high above the ground.

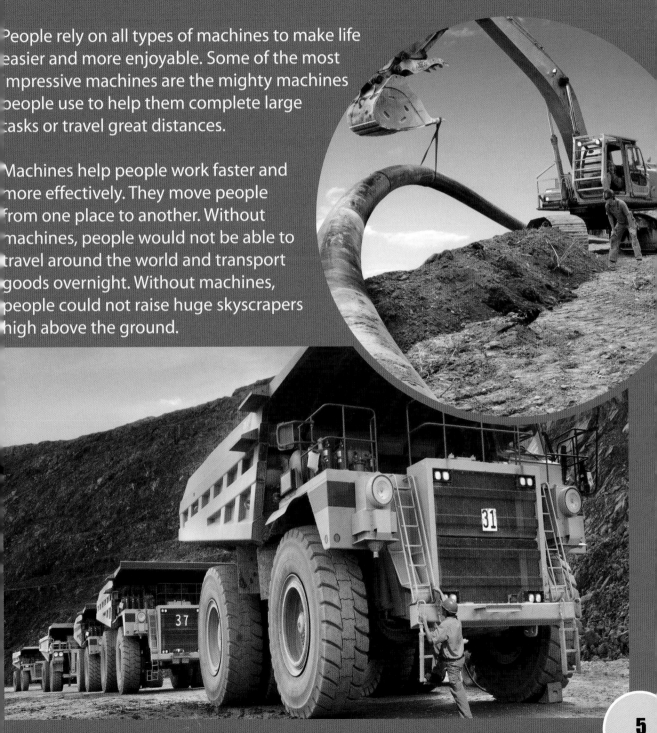

What is a Bulldozer?

A bulldozer can be used to fill holes, flatten ground, or move heavy objects.

Bulldozers can move almost any object. They can rip apart mountains and push rocks and dirt to a new place. The huge blade on the front of a bulldozer moves dirt, rocks, trees, and other objects.

The world's biggest bulldozer weighs more than 22 elephants. It is 16 feet (4.9 meters) tall, 41 feet (12.5 m) long, and 24 feet (7.3 m) wide.

Blade Cylinders
A special system is used to power the blade. This system makes large amounts of energy by squeezing oil from one tube to another. This creates power in a part of the bulldozer that had none before.

Blade
Bulldozers have a large blade on the front. The blade pushes dirt from place to place.

Cab

A driver sits in the cab. The driver controls the bulldozer using **levers**. One lever changes the direction and speed of the bulldozer. A second lever moves the blade up and down.

Engine

Many bulldozers have very powerful engines. The world's biggest bulldozer has enough power to move 485,000 pounds (219,992 kilograms) at one time.

Tracks

Tracks keep bulldozers from sinking on wet, muddy, or sandy ground. They move more easily than wheels across uneven ground.

How to Draw a Bulldozer

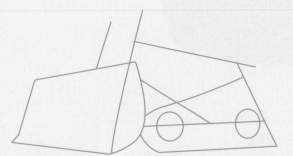

1 Start by drawing a stick figure frame of the bulldozer. Use circles for the wheels, and lines for the blade and body, as shown.

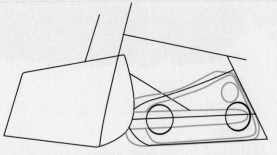

2 Now, draw the metal track around the wheels.

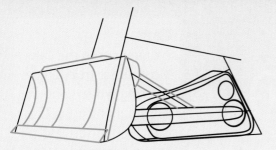

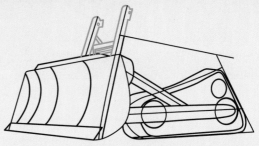

3 Next, draw the blade and blade arms.

4 Now, draw the grill above the blade, and complete the blade cylinders, as shown.

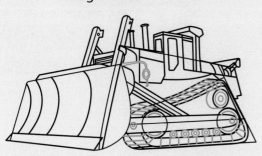

5 In this step, draw the cab and engine using straight lines.

6 Draw the cab shade and pipes, as shown.

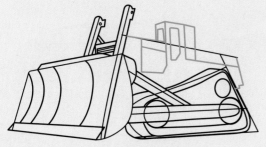

7 Now, draw the headlights, and complete the track by drawing small lines on its surface.

8 Erase the extra lines and the stick figure.

9 Color the picture.

What is a Dump Truck?

Cab
A driver sits in the cab. Most dump trucks have steering wheels, much like smaller trucks. The hopper is raised and lowered with a lever.

Dump trucks move dirt, rocks, and other objects around a work site. These huge machines have a big box on the back that can be filled with objects. The dump truck moves to a new place and dumps the objects out.

The world's biggest dump trucks are so large that they cannot fit on a regular road. These massive trucks are brought to the work site in pieces and put together. Each tire on one of these massive trucks is 13 feet (4 m) tall and weighs 116,800 pounds (52,980 kg).

Engine
Dump trucks have huge engines. These engines have extra power for carrying heavy loads.

Load

Dump trucks can carry many materials, from dirt and rocks to garbage and debris. Whatever a dump truck carries is called the load.

Hopper

The solid metal box on the back of the dump truck keeps the load from falling out. It can tip to pour out its load.

Wheels

A dump truck's tires are made of thick rubber. This allows for huge loads to be placed in the back of a dump truck without ruining the tires.

How to Draw a
Dump Truck

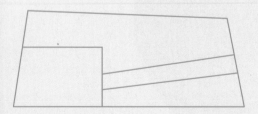
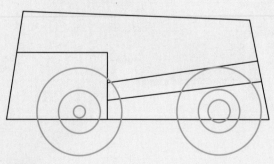

1 Start with a stick figure frame of the dump truck. Draw a rectangle for the body. Then, draw lines inside of the rectangle.

2 Now, draw the wheels.

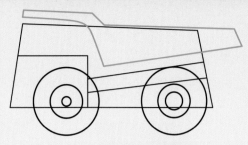

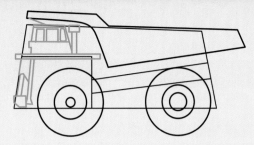

3 Next, draw the hopper using curved and straight lines.

4 Draw the engine and cab with the windows, as shown.

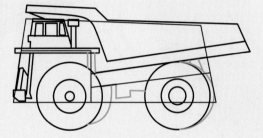

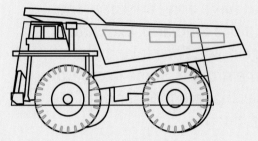

5 In this step, draw the other two wheels and the rest of the truck frame, as shown.

6 Draw small lines on the wheels, and add details to the hopper.

7 Now, draw the rocks in the hopper, as shown.

8 Erase the extra lines and the stick figure.

9 Color the picture.

What is an Excavator?

An excavator is a big machine that has a large bucket at the end of a long arm. Excavators dig huge holes. They take material out of the ground. Some excavators dig holes that are thousands of feet (meters) deep.

The arm of an excavator works like a human arm. The arm has two parts. It moves like a wrist and elbow to guide the bucket. The bucket is like a hand that digs into dirt.

Bucket

Excavators use the bucket to dig holes. Metal teeth at the end of the bucket scrape and dig at the ground. The bucket fills with dirt, rocks, and other objects. When it is full, the driver in the cab swings the arm and dumps the objects.

Stick

The stick is the part of the arm that is attached to the boom. It has a **joint** like a person's elbow. The stick gives the excavator the power to pull the bucket through the dirt.

Cylinders

The cylinders are **hydraulic** systems that move the arm. A hydraulic system pushes oil from one tube to another. This action creates power in another part of the machine.

Boom

The part of the arm closest to the cab is called the boom. Mono booms are only able to move up and down. Knuckle booms can move up and down, as well as left to right.

Cab

The arm is attached to a cab that can spin around. An excavator's cab is called the house, and it sits on top of wheels or tracks.

Tracks

Most excavators have tracks. Tracks are better than wheels for moving on rocky dirt roads. However, track excavators move more slowly than wheel excavators.

How to Draw an Excavator

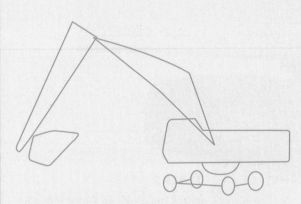

1 Start with a stick figure frame of the excavator. Draw triangles for the boom and stick, circles for the wheels, and lines for the bucket and body.

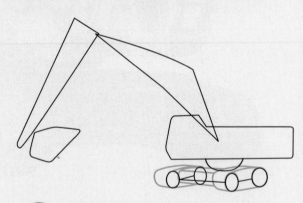

2 Now, draw the track base using curved lines.

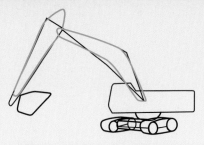

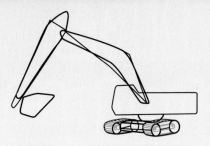

③ Next, draw the boom and stick on the triangles from Step 1, as shown above.

④ Now, add details to the tracks.

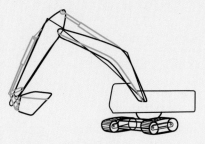

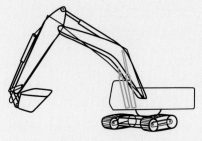

⑤ In this step, complete the bucket, and draw the cylinders.

⑥ Draw the arms supporting the boom and stick using cylinders.

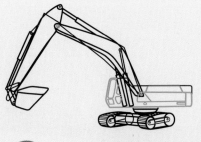

⑦ Now, draw the cab and body with doors and windows, as shown.

⑧ Erase the extra lines and the stick figure.

⑨ Color the picture.

What is a Jumbo Jet?

Jumbo jets are large planes that carry hundreds of people at one time. They also carry large loads of goods from one place to another.

The first jumbo jet was the 747 made by Boeing. It could carry as many as 490 people at once. The largest jumbo jet today is the Airbus A380. This massive machine can carry more than 800 people on one flight. A fully loaded A380 can weigh more than 1 million pounds (453,592 kg).

Flight Deck
The pilots sit in a room called the flight deck, or cockpit. The flight deck is at the front of the jet. It is filled with buttons, knobs, and levers that control the jet.

Wings
The wings of the jet create a force that raises it into the air. High speeds help jets create the forces they need to fly.

Rudder

The rudder turns to move the jet left or right without changing its angle in the air.

Doors

Doors on a jumbo jet allow people to enter and exit the plane. They also often house **inflatable** emergency slides. After an emergency landing, the slides inflate, and people can safely slide to the ground.

Jet Engines

A jet's powerful engines create a force that moves the jet forward. In the air, a jumbo jet can travel more than 600 miles (966 km) per hour.

How to Draw a Jumbo Jet

1 Start with a stick figure frame of the jumbo jet, as shown. Draw a cylindrical shape, a small circle for the body, and lines for the wings.

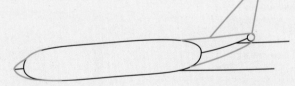

2 Now, join the cylindrical shape and circle with curved lines, and draw the rudder.

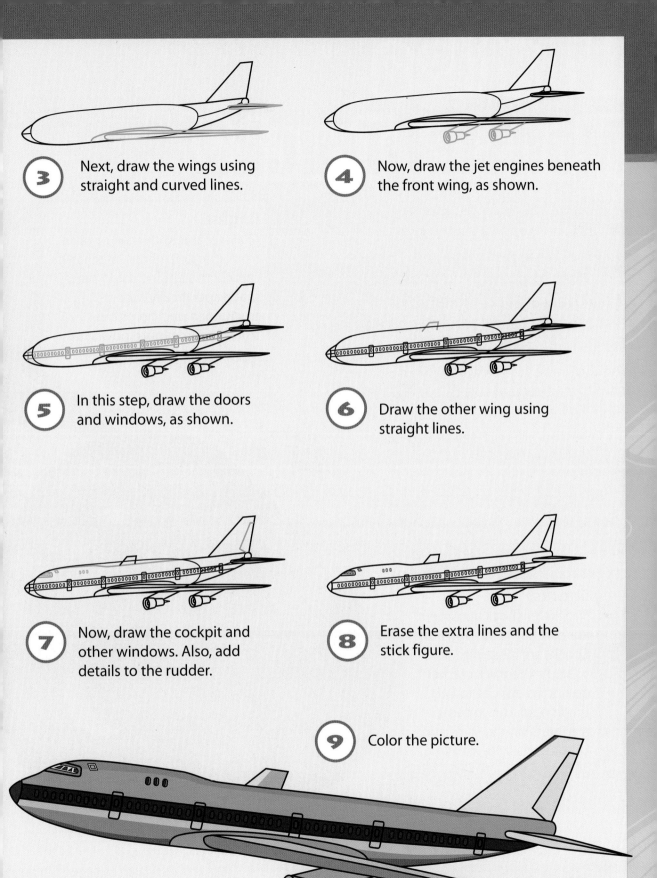

3 Next, draw the wings using straight and curved lines.

4 Now, draw the jet engines beneath the front wing, as shown.

5 In this step, draw the doors and windows, as shown.

6 Draw the other wing using straight lines.

7 Now, draw the cockpit and other windows. Also, add details to the rudder.

8 Erase the extra lines and the stick figure.

9 Color the picture.

What is a Monster Truck?

Monster trucks are often part of large performances. These big trucks with huge wheels drive over cars or climb tall piles of dirt. Monster trucks are also known for jumping over other vehicles. At performances, cars are lined up in a row or stacked on top of each other. Monster trucks jump through the air and crash down on top of the cars.

Engine

Monster trucks get their power from special engines. Mechanics rebuild the engine using parts made specifically for one truck. Each part helps the truck become more powerful.

Shocks

Shocks, or shock absorbers, are part of the **suspension**. Shocks are filled with fluid or air. As the truck crashes down, the shocks absorb the impact. This reduces the stress on the truck and keeps parts from breaking.

Cab

Monster truck drivers sit in the cab. Monster truck cabs are much stronger than a normal truck's cab. They are **reinforced** with metal bars and have **harnesses** for the driver.

Wheels

The wheels on a monster truck are taller than the height of the average woman and almost as wide as a small car.

Decoration

Most monster trucks are decorated with **logos**, colors, and objects, such as horns or spikes.

How to Draw a Monster Truck

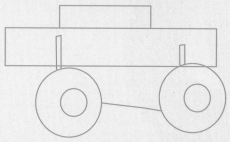

1 Start with a stick figure frame of the monster truck. Use circles for the wheels and rectangles for the body.

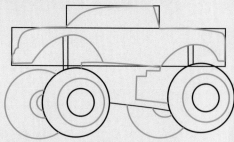

2 Now, draw the body inside the rectangles from the previous step using curved lines. Also, draw the other two wheels using circles.

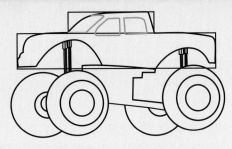

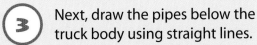

3 Next, draw the pipes below the truck body using straight lines.

4 Now, draw the windows, as shown.

5 In this step, draw the front of the truck with the head lights and engine grill.

6 Draw the engine details, as shown.

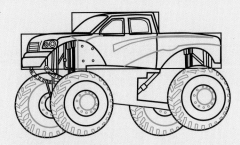

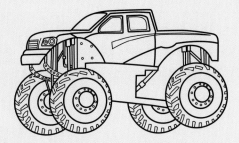

7 Now, draw long curved lines on the body and small curved figures on the wheels.

8 Erase the extra lines and the stick figure.

9 Color the picture.

What is a Tractor?

Tractors are heavy, powerful machines that often work on farms. They help to make work faster and easier. Most tractor work is done off-road. Tractors have been used for more than 100 years.

Other tractors are used by people to construct buildings and roads. Soldiers use armored tractors to build camps and barriers. Tractors even do work at airports. They pull carts of luggage to airplanes.

Engine

A tractor has a big powerful engine. The engine is strong, so the tractor can carry heavy loads. Most tractors have diesel engines. Diesel is a thick, oily fuel.

Cab
Tractor drivers sit inside the cab. The cab protects the driver from dust and noise. Cabs have a sturdy frame. The frame keeps the cab from folding in on the driver if the tractor rolls over.

Wheels
The rear wheels are larger than the front wheels to provide more surface for **traction**. They are also bigger so that the tractor can drive over small holes.

Attachments
Special parts can be attached to tractors to help them do different kinds of work. These attachments can be anything from a shovel to an excavation bucket.

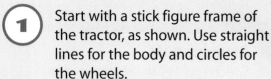

1. Start with a stick figure frame of the tractor, as shown. Use straight lines for the body and circles for the wheels.

2. Now, draw the engine and exhaust pipe using straight lines.

3 Next, draw the fender for the rear wheel, as shown.

4 Now, draw the cab, as shown.

5 In this step, draw the steering wheel and ladder, as shown.

6 Draw the lights and the inner part of the wheels, as shown.

 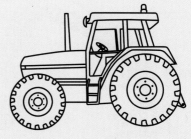

7 Now, draw the rear body of the tractor, and complete the engine. Also, draw small circles in the center and curved figures on the wheels.

8 Erase the extra lines and the stick figure.

9 Color the picture.

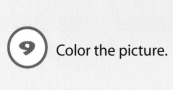

Test Your Knowledge of Machines

1.

The world's biggest bulldozer weighs more than how many elephants?

Answer: 22

2.

A dump truck's box, which carries the load, is called what?

Answer: The hopper

3.

Mono booms can move in what directions?

Answer: Up and down

4.

The first jumbo jet was made by what company?

Answer: Boeing

5.

What are monster trucks often decorated with?

Answer: Logos, colors, and objects, such as horns or spikes

6.

How long have tractors been used?

Answer: More than 100 years

Want to learn more? Log on to av2books.com to access more content.

Draw an Environment

Materials
- Large white poster board
- Internet connection or library
- Pencils and crayons or markers
- Glue or tape

Steps
1. Complete one of the machine drawings in this book. Cut out the drawing.
2. Using this book, the internet, and a library, find out about your machine and the environment in which it works.
3. Think about the environment where machines work. What does its environment look like? What sorts of trees are there? Is there water? What does the landscape look like? Are there other machines in its environment? What kinds of work are the machines doing? What other important features might you find in the machine's environment?
4. On the large white poster board, draw an environment for your machine. Be sure to place all the features you noted in step 3.
5. Place the cutout machine in its environment with glue or tape. Color the machine's environment to complete the activity.

Glossary

communication: the sending and receiving of information

harnesses: safety straps that keep a driver in the seat

hydraulic: a system that creates power by squeezing a liquid through tubes

imagination: the ability to form new creative ideas or images

inflatable: can be filled with air

joint: the point where different parts of a machine are joined together

levers: bars or rods that control parts of a machine

logos: a picture that represents a company or organization

reinforced: strengthened with a strong material

suspension: a system of springs and shocks that cushion a vehicle from rough terrain

traction: the grip of a tire on a surface

Log on to www.av2books.com

AV² by Weigl brings you media enhanced books that support active learning. Go to www.av2books.com, and enter the special code found on page 2 of this book. You will gain access to enriched and enhanced content that supplements and complements this book. Content includes video, audio, web links, quizzes, a slide show, and activities.

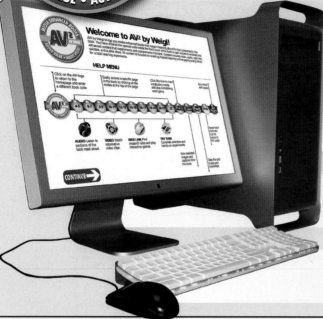

Audio
Listen to sections of the book read aloud.

Video
Watch informative video clips.

Embedded Weblinks
Gain additional information for research.

Try This!
Complete activities and hands-on experiments.

WHAT'S ONLINE?

Try This!	Embedded Weblinks	Video	**EXTRA FEATURES**
Complete an interactive drawing tutorial for each of the six machines in the book.	Learn more about each of the six machines in the book.	Watch a video about machines.	**Audio** Listen to sections of the book read aloud.
			Key Words Study vocabulary, and complete a matching word activity.
			Slide Show View images and captions and prepare a presentation
			Quizzes Test your knowledge.

AV² was built to bridge the gap between print and digital. We encourage you to tell us what you like and what you want to see in the future.

Sign up to be an AV² Ambassador at www.av2books.com/ambassador.